HOW TO START A CORPORATE WELLNESS PROGRAM

TECHNIQUES FOR STARTING CORPORATE WELLNESS PROGRAM

CYRIL LAKES

Contents

CHAPTER ONE 3

INTRODUCTION 3

    Corporate wellness programs are important 5

    Recognizing the Advantages of Workplace Wellness Initiatives 10

CHAPTER TWO 16

    Evaluating the Goals and Needs of the Organization 16

    Choosing Program Objectives and Measures 22

    Creating All-Inclusive Wellness Programs 28

    Increasing Buy-In and Support from Leadership 35

    Program Implementation and Evaluation 41

CHAPTER THREE 43

    Encouraging Participation and Engagement among Workers .. 51

    Providing Assistance and Resources 57

CHAPTER FOUR 61

    Taking Inclusion and Equity Into Account 65

    Summary 71

THE END 75

CHAPTER ONE

INTRODUCTION

The health of employees is becoming more and more important in today's hectic work environment for an organization to succeed. Realizing this, a growing number of businesses are using corporate wellness initiatives to promote the wellbeing and health of their employees. These initiatives go above and beyond standard healthcare benefits in an effort to foster a healthy culture that boosts worker retention, productivity, and engagement.

Establishing a corporate wellness program is a wise business move that can have a big impact on employees' health in addition to being a proactive investment in their well-being. Businesses may lower healthcare expenses, lower absenteeism, boost morale, and create a great work environment by putting employee well-being first.

We will go over the important procedures and factors to take into account while launching a business wellness program in this article. This guide will offer you useful insights and strategies to build a program that promotes employee health and happiness while boosting organizational performance and success, from identifying the needs of your workforce to creating and executing customized wellness initiatives.

Corporate wellness programs are important

In today's workplace, corporate wellness programs are essential since they provide a wealth of advantages to both businesses and employees. This is a summary of their significance:

Better Worker Health: Corporate wellness efforts put a premium on worker health by providing tools and activities that support mental, emotional, and physical health. Among other things, these programs frequently include stress management courses, dietary counseling, fitness challenges, health examinations, and assistance in quitting smoking. Companies may minimize healthcare expenses, improve general well-being, and lower the risk of chronic diseases by investing in the health of their employees.

Enhanced output: Workers in good health are more efficient. Employees who participate in wellness programs report feeling more focused and concentrated, have more energy, and perform better overall. Businesses can foster a high-achieving and performance-oriented work atmosphere by offering services to enhance the well-being of their employees.

Increased Employee Engagement: Corporate wellness initiatives show workers that their employers are concerned about their well-being, which fosters a higher level of engagement and loyalty. Employees are more likely to feel appreciated and dedicated to their company if they receive assistance in their wellness initiatives. Additionally, motivated workers are more likely to go above and beyond, offer creative solutions, and work well with others.

Decreased Absenteeism: Well-being makes it less likely for workers to skip work due to illness or accidents. Employee adoption of healthier lifestyles can result in lower absenteeism and higher attendance rates when corporate wellness programs are implemented. Businesses can reduce the negative effects of illness and absenteeism on workflow and production by supporting preventive care and healthy habits.

Reduced Healthcare Costs: Businesses can save a lot of money by making investments in the health and wellness of their workforce.

Companies can lower healthcare expenses related to medical treatments, hospital stays, and prescription medication by supporting healthy lifestyle choices, promoting preventive care, and avoiding and treating chronic conditions. Furthermore, healthier workers are less likely to need medical treatment and make insurance claims, which saves companies money over time.

Better Workplace Culture: Workplace wellness initiatives can support the development of a happy, healthy, and work-life balanced work environment. Wellness activities can foster a feeling of community inside the firm and build employee relationships by encouraging camaraderie, teamwork, and mutual support. Retention rates, job satisfaction, and employee morale can all be raised by a positive workplace culture.

Attractive Benefit for Employees: Providing a corporate wellness program can improve an organization's appeal to potential employees. In the current competitive labor market, job seekers frequently look for companies that place a high value on employee well-being and provide extensive benefit plans. A strong wellness program can be an effective tool for recruiting and employee retention, assisting businesses in attracting top talent and keeping their finest workers for an extended period of time.

All things considered, organizations that are healthier, happier, and more engaged must have corporate wellness programs. Businesses can gain a lot from investing in the health and well-being of their workforce, including increased productivity, decreased absenteeism, cheaper healthcare expenses, and better employee satisfaction and retention.

Recognizing the Advantages of Workplace Wellness Initiatives

Programs for corporate wellness have several advantages for both businesses and employees. Here's a thorough analysis of the benefits they offer:

Better Worker Health: Corporate wellness activities, such as fitness challenges, stress management seminars, health screenings, and nutrition education, are designed to improve worker health and wellbeing. These programs can lower the risk of chronic diseases, improve overall health outcomes, and increase the vitality and longevity of employees by promoting healthy behaviors and lifestyles.

Enhanced output: Workers in good health are more efficient. Employees who participate in wellness programs report feeling more focused and concentrated, have more energy, and perform better overall. Businesses can establish a work environment that stimulates high levels of engagement, creativity, and innovation by offering tools and assistance for the well-being of their employees.

Decreased absence: The production and operations of a firm can be greatly impacted by employee absence resulting from illness or accident. By encouraging healthy habits, promoting preventative care, and offering resources for managing chronic disorders, corporate wellness programs can help lower absenteeism. Employers can reduce the disturbance caused by unscheduled absences and preserve workflow and operations by maintaining resilient and healthy staff.

Reduce Healthcare expenses: As healthcare expenses keep going up, both businesses and employees are facing financial difficulties. By managing and preventing chronic illnesses, lowering the need for medical care and hospital stays, and encouraging preventive care and good lifestyle choices, corporate wellness initiatives can contribute to lower healthcare expenditures. Businesses may increase profitability and cut costs over the long run by making investments in the health and wellness of their workforce.

Increased Employee Engagement: Wellness initiatives show workers that their companies are concerned about their health and well-being, which boosts employee engagement, loyalty, and dedication. Employees that are engaged are more likely to go above and beyond in their jobs, offer creative solutions, and work well with others. Establishing a wellness and health-oriented culture can help businesses improve employee morale, job satisfaction, and retention rates.

Better Workplace Culture: Work-life balance, comradery, and mutual support are characteristics of a positive workplace culture, which can be enhanced by corporate wellness initiatives. Businesses can give workers chances to interact, network, and form relationships outside of work by supporting wellness programs and events. An organization's sense of community and belonging can be fostered, morale can be raised, and teamwork can be improved with a healthy workplace culture.

Enticing Benefit for Employees: Providing a corporate wellness program can increase an organization's appeal as an employer. In the current competitive job market, jobseekers frequently take wellness programs and other employee benefits into account when assessing job options. A strong wellness program can be an effective tool for recruiting and employee retention, assisting businesses in attracting top talent and keeping their finest workers for an extended period of time.

In general, corporate wellness initiatives have a lot to offer both companies and employees. Businesses may achieve measurable business benefits like higher productivity, decreased absenteeism, and lower healthcare expenses while also building healthier, happier, and more engaged workplaces by investing in the health and well-being of their workforce.

CHAPTER TWO

Evaluating the Goals and Needs of the Organization

An essential first step in launching a corporate wellness program is assessing the needs and goals of the firm. You may effectively meet the requirements of your workforce and accomplish desired outcomes by customizing your wellness initiatives to your organization's specific issues, objectives, and goals. Here's ways to evaluate the goals and needs of an organization:

Employee Surveys: To find out more about the present health state, wellness needs, interests, and preferences of your staff, start by conducting surveys or focus groups. Inquire about their work-life balance, stress levels, mental and physical health, and desire in taking part in wellness activities.

Examine Health Data: To find common health problems and patterns within your company, examine the health data that is currently available, such as insurance claims, absenteeism rates, and employee assistance program usage. Examine data to identify problem areas and possible areas for development in areas including ergonomics, stress management, and the management of chronic diseases.

Examine Organizational Culture: Determine the degree of support for employee well-being by assessing the workplace culture and organizational culture. Take into account elements like the dedication of the leadership, communication styles, work-life balance guidelines, and the resources available for health promotion programs.

Determine Important Stakeholders: Determine the important individuals within the company who will be engaged in the wellness program's development, execution, and supervision. Senior management, human resources, benefit administrators, occupational health specialists, and employee reps are a few examples of this.

Examine Business aims: Make sure the wellness program's aims are in line with the organization's larger business goals and priorities. Examine the ways in which enhancing employee health and well-being can support strategic objectives including raising employee engagement, cutting healthcare costs, boosting productivity, or strengthening company culture.

Benchmarking Your Organization's Wellness Efforts Against Industry Standards: To determine how you stack up against peers and competitors, benchmark your organization's wellness initiatives against industry standards and best practices. To determine your program's strengths and opportunities for development, compare its wellness offers, features, and participation rates.

Think About Legal and Regulatory Requirements: Take into account any legal and regulatory requirements, such as privacy laws, anti-discrimination legislation, and Affordable

Care Act standards, that may have an impact on the development and execution of your wellness program. To reduce legal concerns, make sure your program conforms with all applicable rules and regulations.

Obtain Leadership Input: Speak with top leadership to ensure that the wellness program has support and buy-in. Make the leadership aware of the possible advantages of funding employee health and well-being, and ask for their opinion on the program's strategic aims and intended results.

Define Specific Goals: After reviewing the results of your needs analysis, make sure your wellness program has specific, quantifiable goals. Establish clear objectives for enhancing the health of employees, lowering risk factors, raising engagement rates, and attaining corporate objectives like cost savings or increased productivity.

Prioritize Initiatives: Set the order of importance for wellness initiatives in accordance with your organization's goals and demands. Concentrate on programs that address the most urgent health issues, fit in with organizational aims, and have the biggest chance of improving the health and wellbeing of staff members.

You can create a focused and successful corporate wellness program that meets the particular requirements and priorities of your workforce and advances the strategic objectives of your company by thoroughly evaluating the needs and goals of your firm.

Choosing Program Objectives and Measures

A business wellness program's design, execution, and assessment must be guided by the establishment of precise program goals and measures. Here's how to successfully set program objectives and metrics:

Align with Organizational aims: To begin, make sure that the wellness program's aims are in line with the organization's larger priorities and objectives. Examine the ways in which enhancing employee health and well-being can support strategic objectives including raising employee engagement, cutting healthcare costs, boosting productivity, or strengthening company culture.

Be Measurable and Specific: Establish goals that are quantifiable and explicit, outlining your objectives for the wellness program. For instance, instead of aiming for a general purpose like "improve employee health," establish more focused goals like "reduce absenteeism by 15%" or "increase participation in wellness activities by 20%."

Use SMART Criteria: When establishing program goals, take into account the SMART criteria (Specific, Measurable, Achievable, Relevant, Time-bound). Make sure your objectives are clear, quantifiable, doable in a reasonable amount of time, pertinent to organizational priorities, and consistent with the program's overarching vision.

Think About Wellness's Many Aspects: Well-being has many facets, including mental, emotional, physical, social, and even financial. Establish objectives that cover several aspects of wellbeing to develop a thorough and all-encompassing program that promotes workers' general well-being.

Put an emphasis on Results: Establish outcome-based measurements to gauge how the wellness program affects worker health, output, and overall organizational success. Changes in health indicators (e.g., blood pressure, cholesterol levels), decreases in healthcare expenditures, enhancements in employee engagement ratings, or gains in productivity metrics are a few examples of outcome metrics.

Add Process and Participation Metrics: Track program implementation and engagement levels with process and participation metrics in addition to outcome indicators. The quantity of wellness activities available, program participation rates, health screening completion rates, and resource utilization rates are examples of process metrics.

Establish Baseline Data: To give a point of reference for tracking advancement and assessing the wellness program's efficacy over time, establish baseline data for each indicator. Prior to program implementation, gather baseline data from relevant sources such as health evaluations, employee surveys, claims data, and other sources.

Establish Success Criteria: To ascertain what qualifies as successful accomplishment, clearly establish success criteria for each program goal and measure. Determine benchmarks or target thresholds that signify successful results, and establish reasonable expectations for what can be accomplished in the allotted time.

Monitor and Track Progress: Put in place the procedures and systems necessary to routinely monitor and track program objectives and metrics. To get, examine, and display data on program performance and results, use dashboards, reporting systems, tracking software, and data gathering tools.

Evaluate and Adjust: Constantly assess program performance in relation to predetermined objectives and KPIs. Apply the knowledge gained from evaluation results to decision-making and program modification. To keep the wellness program efficient and adaptable to the changing demands of the workforce and the company, pinpoint areas of success, areas for development, and chances for improvement.

Organizations may successfully monitor the effectiveness of their corporate wellness programs, show return on investment, and make data-driven decisions to improve employee health, well-being, and organizational performance by setting clear program goals and measurements.

Creating All-Inclusive Wellness Programs

A crucial first step in launching a business wellness program is creating all-encompassing wellness programs. These programs should focus on important aspects of health and well-being and be customized to the unique requirements, passions, and preferences of your employees. For your workplace wellness program, consider the following when creating complete wellness initiatives:

Perform a Needs Assessment: To determine the health-related needs, obstacles, and priorities of your workforce, begin with a comprehensive needs assessment. To learn more about the interests, preferences, and current health status of your employees, conduct focus groups, questionnaires, or health assessments and get their input.

Decide on Important Areas of Focus: Choose important areas of focus for your wellness initiatives based on the results of the needs assessment. Physical fitness, diet, stress management, mental health, quitting smoking, sleep hygiene, ergonomics, and preventative care are examples of common areas.

Provide a Variety of Programs: To cater to employees with different interests and preferences, create a wide selection of wellness programs and initiatives. Provide a range of wellness-related programs, including physical fitness courses, dietary seminars, mindfulness exercises, smoking cessation aids, and health examinations.

Encourage Preventive treatment: To address health concerns and advance general well-being, place a strong emphasis on early intervention and preventive treatment. To assist staff members in recognizing and proactively managing health concerns, provide routine health screenings, immunizations, flu shots, and preventative health check-ups.

Encourage staff to Incorporate Movement Into Daily Routines: Encourage staff to engage in physical activity. Provide exercise classes onsite, walking groups, fitness challenges, or rewards for taking part in physical activity programs.

Provide Nutrition knowledge: To assist staff in choosing better foods and developing balanced eating habits, provide them with resources and knowledge on nutrition. Make healthy recipe ideas, cooking demos, nutrition workshops, and advice on portion control and meal planning accessible.

Supporting Mental Health and Stress Management: Take steps to support mental health and stress management by offering counseling services, employee assistance programs, stress reduction courses, mindfulness training, and meditation sessions. Establish a welcoming environment where staff members can come to you for support when they need it with mental health concerns.

Encourage Work-Life Balance: To foster work-life balance, provide telecommuting opportunities, flexible work schedules, and rules that promote taking time off for leisure and relaxation. Give staff members the tools and resources they need to prioritize their work, manage their workloads, and draw boundaries between their personal and professional lives.

Integrate Financial Wellness: To assist staff in managing financial stress and enhancing their financial literacy, think about integrating financial wellness programs into your wellness program. Organize seminars on saving techniques, retirement planning, debt management, and budgeting.

Leverage Technology: Make better use of technology to improve the accessibility and delivery of wellness programs. Think about using wearable technology, smartphone apps, or wellness platforms to monitor progress, provide staff feedback, and encourage involvement.

Encourage a Culture of Wellness: Make wellness a part of the workplace culture by incorporating wellbeing into everyday operations. Motivate the leadership to promote wellness initiatives, publicly support them, and acknowledge and celebrate the accomplishments and engagement of your staff.

Evaluate and Adjust: Regularly assess the success of your wellness programs and make necessary changes in response to input and the results of your evaluation. Track results, engagement levels, and participation rates to pinpoint areas that need work and gradually enhance program approaches.

You may develop a corporate wellness program that supports worker productivity, health, and well-being by creating all-encompassing wellness activities that cater to the many requirements and interests of your staff. Initiatives that are customized to individual health objectives and preferences will increase involvement and engagement, which will benefit the firm and its workforce in the long run.

Increasing Buy-In and Support from Leadership

Establishing support and getting leadership buy-in are essential components of a business wellness program's effective launch. Here's how to win over important stakeholders and win their commitment:

Educate Leadership: Begin by informing important decision-makers and senior leadership about the advantages of business wellness initiatives. Emphasize the possible return on investment, such as better worker health, more output, decreased absenteeism, and cheaper medical expenses. Present case studies, empirical research, and success stories from other firms to demonstrate how wellness initiatives affect business outcomes.

Align with Organizational Goals: Stress how the organization's mission, values, and strategic objectives are in line with the corporate wellness program. Clearly state how funding employee health and wellbeing contributes to overarching corporate objectives including raising employee engagement, luring and keeping talent, and cultivating a happy work environment.

Show ROI: Provide statistics and data that illustrate the wellness program's possible return on investment. To determine the financial return on investment from investing in employee wellness, use cost-benefit assessments, financial predictions, and prospective savings computations. Emphasize the long-term benefits of health promotion and preventive care programs in lowering medical expenses and enhancing organizational effectiveness.

Involve Middle Management: Obtain the backing of department heads and middle managers, who are essential in promoting employee involvement in wellness programs. Inform managers of the wellness program's advantages and solicit their assistance in fostering and advancing employee participation. Give managers the tools and training they need to convince their teams of the benefits of wellness programs.

Engage HR and Benefits Teams: Work together with the HR and benefits teams to include wellness programs into the current policies and programs for employees. Utilize the knowledge and skills of HR specialists to create, execute, and oversee wellness initiatives. Ensure that these initiatives are in line with employee benefit plans and health insurance options.

Make a Business Case: Construct a strong business case that details the goals, justification, and anticipated results of the corporate wellness initiative. Clearly state the requirement of funding employee health and wellbeing, name the target audiences, and list the tactics and tools needed to carry out the program. To gain their support and commitment, provide the business case to senior leadership and decision-makers.

Create a Coalition of Champions: To help the program get traction and support, assemble a coalition of wellness advocates and champions from around the company. Find key personnel who have a strong interest in health and wellness and ask them to help spread the word about the initiative, create excitement, and motivate colleagues to participate.

Effective Communication: Create a thorough communication strategy to spread the word about the workplace wellness program and create excitement. Use a variety of communication channels to tell staff members about program offers, benefits, and forthcoming events, including staff meetings, email, newsletters, and intranet announcements. Make it obvious how the leadership will support the program and boost staff involvement.

Handle Objections and Concerns: Be prepared for and respond to any objections or concerns that stakeholders may have about how the wellness program is being implemented. Be open and honest about the program's objectives, requirements, and any difficulties. You should also offer chances for discussion and feedback to allay any fears or doubts.

Start Small and Scale Up: To provide proof of concept and progressively gain traction, think about beginning with a pilot program or phased rollout. Start small and gradually increase the number of health programs or events in response to participant feedback, degree of participation, and proven results. Make the most of your early successes to secure more funding and support for expanding the program.

You can ensure continued commitment and investment in the health and well-being of your employees and lay a solid basis for success by garnering support and leadership buy-in for the corporate wellness program. Driving corporate support and engagement in wellness initiatives requires involving key stakeholders, showcasing the program's value proposition, and clearly communicating its advantages.

Program Implementation and Evaluation

The implementation and assessment of wellness programs are crucial phases in guaranteeing their efficacy and influence on the health and welfare of employees. Here are some tips for putting business wellness programs into action and assessing their effectiveness:

Putting Wellness Programs Into Practice:

Make an Implementation Plan: Draft a thorough implementation plan that specifies the duties, deadlines, materials, and tasks necessary to properly introduce the wellness program. outline clear lines of communication, assign roles and duties to program participants, and outline reasonable goals and objectives for the program's execution.

CHAPTER THREE

Choose Wellness Initiatives: Choose a range of wellness initiatives and activities to incorporate into the program based on the needs assessment and program objectives. Think about providing a variety of activities that touch on several aspects of wellbeing, including diet, stress reduction, mental health, physical fitness, and preventive care.

Involve Employees: To encourage ownership and participation, actively involve employees in the planning and execution of wellness initiatives. Utilize focus groups, surveys, or wellness committees to get input, thoughts, and suggestions from staff members to make sure that initiatives are inclusive, timely, and appealing to workers.

Increase Program Awareness: To encourage awareness and engagement in the wellness program, create a thorough communication plan. When educating staff members about program options, advantages, and forthcoming events, use a variety of communication channels, including social media, email, newsletters, intranet announcements, and posters.

Provide Tools and Resources: Employees can engage in wellness activities and meet their health objectives with the assistance of tools, resources, and support. Provide wellness workshops, health examinations, exercise centers, internet tools, and incentives or prizes for participation and accomplishment.

Provide Accessibility and Flexibility: Acknowledge that workers have a range of schedules, needs, and preferences. To accommodate varying work arrangements, shift patterns, and personal obligations, provide flexibility in program offerings, scheduling, and delivery methods. To ensure that all employees may participate, offer both onsite and remote options.

Develop Program Facilitators: To effectively implement wellness initiatives and encourage employee involvement, develop program facilitators, coordinators, and wellness champions. Give instruction on the objectives of the program, its substance, its administration, its communication tactics, and its best practices for advancing health and wellbeing.

Assessing Wellbeing Initiatives:

Establish Evaluation Criteria: To gauge the success and influence of the wellness program, clearly define and quantifiable evaluation criteria should be established. Determine outcome measurements, benchmarks, and key performance indicators (KPIs) to assess program success and advancement toward objectives.

Gather Baseline Data: Prior to putting the wellness program into action, gather baseline data on pertinent metrics, such as employee health indicators, participation rates, engagement levels, and program expenses. To obtain baseline data, use surveys, health evaluations, claims data, and other sources.

Program Implementation Monitoring: Keep an eye on the way wellness programs and activities are carried out to make sure they follow the plan and are in line with the objectives of the program. To evaluate program engagement and reach, keep track of participation rates, attendance, and the use of wellness tools and services.

Analyze Program Outcomes: Examine program results and effects by recording changes over time and comparing post-program data with baseline data. Track alterations in health indicators for employees, including biometric assessments, health-related behaviors, productivity evaluations, absenteeism rates, and medical expenses.

Collect Feedback: To find out how the wellness program is perceived, what the employees are satisfied with, and what their experiences have been, ask them using surveys, focus groups, or feedback forms. Utilize input to pinpoint program design, execution, and delivery areas that need work as well as its strong points and shortcomings.

Analyze Data and Results: Examine evaluation data to determine program efficacy, spot patterns, and gain understanding of how wellness initiatives affect workers' health and happiness. Reports, dashboards, and data visualization tools can be used to convey findings and outcomes with important stakeholders.

Make Data-Driven Decisions: Based on evaluation results, decide on program modifications, additions, and resource allocation using data. In future program iterations, think about expanding or duplicating effective tactics and interventions that have produced favorable results.

Continuous Improvement: To guarantee the wellness program's continued efficacy and applicability, keep an eye on it and evaluate it frequently. Utilize assessment data to guide future program cycle strategic planning, innovation, and program refinement. Encourage an organization-wide culture of learning and continual development by involving stakeholders in the evaluation process.

Organizations may foster a culture of health and well-being that promotes employee engagement, productivity, and organizational success by successfully implementing and assessing wellness programs. Organizations may maximize the impact of wellness initiatives on employee health outcomes and company success by identifying areas for improvement, optimizing program implementation, and implementing regular evaluation and feedback loops.

Encouraging Participation and Engagement among Workers

Promoting involvement and engagement among employees is crucial to a business wellness program's success. The following tactics can be used to motivate staff members to actively participate in wellness initiatives:

Benefits of the Program: Make sure staff members understand the advantages of taking part in the wellness program. Emphasize how wellness programs may raise employees' performance, productivity, and job satisfaction while also improving their health, well-being, and quality of life.

Provide a captivating Storyline: Craft a storyline and vision for the wellness program that will entice staff members to participate. Explain the company's dedication to the health and well-being of its employees and how the program fits in with its priorities and core values.

Offer Incentives and prizes: To promote engagement in wellness activities, provide incentives and prizes. When offering rewards for completing health exams, taking part in fitness challenges, attending seminars, or reaching health objectives, think about giving out gift cards, goods, wellness program points, or recognition prizes.

Provide Flexible Options: Acknowledge that workers come in a variety of needs, schedules, and preferences. Provide a range of wellness programs and events to suit individuals with varying interests, capacities, and lifestyles. Offer choices for both remote and onsite participation, along with flexible scheduling to meet different work arrangements.

Encourage Peer Support: Provide chances for staff members to participate in wellness activities with one another in order to foster social connections and peer support. Walking clubs, group exercise courses, team-based competitions, and wellness committees can all help to build a feeling of community and camaraderie.

Offer Educational Resources: Give staff members the knowledge and resources they need to take charge of their own health and wellbeing. Give them access to webinars, workshops, lunch-and-learn events, and online resources on subjects like preventive care, stress management, exercise, nutrition, and mental health.

Lead by Example: Encouraging employee involvement in wellness initiatives requires the support and involvement of the leadership team. Senior executives should be urged to show their support for the program, actively engage in wellness events, and set an example of good behavior.

Communicate differently: Tailor messages and channels of communication to appeal to the various demographics and preferences of your workforce. Employ a range of communication methods to reach staff members in different departments, locations, and work shifts, including social media, email, newsletters, intranet, and posters.

Provide Tailored assistance: Assist staff members in establishing and accomplishing their health objectives by offering tailored assistance and advice. To assist staff members in achieving wellness, provide one-on-one coaching, health tests, customized wellness programs, or access to medical specialists.

Celebrate Success: Honor staff members' accomplishments and wellness program milestones. Celebrate both individual and group achievements, tell success stories, and thank participants in public for their dedication, advancement, and improved health.

Get Input and Feedback: Ask staff members about their impressions of the wellness program and any recommendations they may have for enhancements. Provide staff members the chance to submit feedback via surveys, focus groups, or other channels, and then utilize their comments to improve program offerings and employee engagement.

Establish a Supportive Environment: Encourage a welcoming, inclusive workplace where staff members feel appreciated, respected, and encouraged to pursue their wellness goals. Foster an environment of open communication, offer tools for stress management and work-life balance, and encourage a culture of health and wellbeing across the entire company.

By putting these tactics into practice, businesses may foster a culture of health and wellbeing that inspires staff members to take an active role in corporate wellness programs. Through the provision of incentives, flexible work arrangements, peer support, and a friendly work environment, employers may enable their workforce to take charge of their health and well-being and realize benefits for both the individual and the company.

Providing Assistance and Resources

Encouraging participation in and successful execution of a business wellness program requires providing tools and support. The following are some efficient methods for offering assistance and resources when launching a workplace wellness program:

Provide educational tools and resources to staff members so they can learn about many facets of wellness and health. Provide booklets, pamphlets, posters, and digital resources with information on mental health, physical exercise, stress management, diet, and other pertinent subjects.

Online Wellness Portals: Establish an online platform or portal for wellness where staff members may obtain tools, resources, and data about health and wellness. Incorporate features like wellness challenges, health evaluations, articles, films, recipes, and interactive tools for creating goals and monitoring your progress.

Wellness Workshops and Seminars: Organize lunch-and-learn sessions, wellness workshops, and seminars to inform staff members about health-related issues and offer doable advice for enhancing wellbeing. Invite outside experts, medical professionals, or in-house specialists to provide talks on subjects including work-life balance, mindfulness, stress management, fitness, and nutrition.

Fitness Centers and Classes: To promote physical activity and exercise among employees, provide access to on-site fitness centers, exercise classes, or wellness initiatives. To meet a range of interests and fitness levels, provide a choice of fitness options, such as yoga, Pilates, Zumba, strength training, or aerobic workouts.

Health Screenings and Assessments: To assist staff in tracking their health and identifying possible risk factors or health concerns, provide health screenings, assessments, and preventive care services. Offer free or heavily discounted examinations for body composition, blood pressure, cholesterol, glucose, and other important health indicators on-site.

Nutrition Support: Provide information and assistance with nutrition to help staff members choose better foods and change their eating habits. Make healthy cooking demos, meal planning guidelines, nutrition counseling, dietitian consultations, and resources for comprehending food labels and portion proportions available to everyone.

CHAPTER FOUR

Employee Assistance Program (EAP): Provide access to an EAP that offers private counseling, resources, and assistance for dealing with personal and professional issues. Make sure staff members are informed about the EAP and how to use its resources for problems like stress, anxiety, depression, drug misuse, or money worries.

Health Coaching: Offer health coaching services to assist staff members in establishing and accomplishing their wellness and health objectives. Provide one-on-one coaching sessions with wellness experts or licensed health coaches who can offer individualized direction, inspiration, and accountability.

Wellness Challenges and Incentives: To encourage and include staff members in healthy activities, arrange wellness challenges, contests, or incentive schemes. Give provide incentives, prizes, or acknowledgement for involvement, reaching health objectives, or seeing an improvement in health outcomes.

Flexible Work Schedules: Encourage work-life balance and allow time for personal wellness activities by providing flexible work schedules that support employee well-being. Allow employees to prioritize their health requirements by offering options like telecommuting, reduced workweeks, flexible scheduling, or on-site wellness breaks.

Peer Support and Networking: Provide chances for employees to connect, exchange experiences, and support one another's wellness objectives through peer support and networking. To encourage a feeling of community and camaraderie, establish wellness committees, employee resource groups, or social networks centered around health and wellbeing.

Frequent Information and Updates: Provide regular information and updates regarding wellness program offers, events, and resources to keep staff members aware and involved. Make use of a variety of communication platforms, including social media, email, newsletters, the intranet, and posters, to inform staff members about the resources and assistance that are accessible.

Employers can enable staff members to take charge of their health and well-being and actively engage in corporate wellness programs by offering a wide range of resources and support services. Organizations may foster a culture of health and well-being that promotes the resilience and general success of their workforce by providing incentives, counseling services, education, access to facilities, and flexible work schedules.

Taking Inclusion and Equity Into Account

Ensuring that a business wellness program is comprehensive, relevant, and accessible to all employees requires addressing equality and inclusion. Here's how to develop a corporate wellness program that takes fairness and inclusion into account:

Perform a Diversity and Inclusion evaluation: To begin with, carry out an evaluation to learn about the particular requirements, inclinations, and obstacles that various employee demographics inside the company confront. Take into account variables including ability, sexual orientation, age, gender, race, ethnicity, cultural background, and socioeconomic level.

Make Sure There's Representation: Make sure the wellness program is inclusive and reflective of the various needs and experiences that the workforce has to offer. In order to guarantee that the program meets the demands of every employee, incorporate a variety of viewpoints during the planning, decision-making, and execution phases.

Provide Culturally Relevant Programming: Make health initiatives and activities cognizant of the varied experiences and backgrounds of your staff members. They should also be sensitive to cultural differences. In order to make sure that every employee feels appreciated and involved, provide programming that takes into account the cultural preferences, customs, and values of various employee groups.

Language Accessibility: To accommodate employees who may speak English as a second language or have low English proficiency, make sure that wellness program information, communications, and resources are available in several languages. As appropriate, offer language support or translation services to make sure all staff members have access to and understanding of program materials.

Accessibility for Workers with Disabilities: Make certain that the resources, activities, and facilities of the wellness program are available to workers with disabilities. To guarantee that every employee can fully participate, take into account accessibility needs including wheelchair access, assistive technology, sign language interpretation, and alternative formats for program materials.

Provide Flexible Options: To meet the needs, preferences, and schedules of diverse individuals, offer flexible options for engaging in wellness activities. Provide a selection of program schedules, forms, and delivery techniques (onsite, remote, virtual, etc.) to make sure that staff members with different work schedules and personal obligations may access it.

Handle Financial Barriers: Take into account the costs associated with engaging in wellness activities and make sure that they don't prevent people from doing so. Provide free or inexpensive wellness programs, discounts or subsidies for wellness initiatives, and financial support for staff members who might have trouble affording to participate.

Encourage Inclusive Language and Messaging: In all correspondence and marketing materials pertaining to the wellness program, use inclusive language and messaging. Steer clear of any rhetoric that might be interpreted as discriminating or exclusive, and work to make the workplace a friendly place for all workers.

Provide Training and Education: Provide program managers, staff members, and leaders with training and instruction on diversity, equity, and inclusion-related subjects. Offer information, instruments, and direction on how to establish welcoming environments, encourage a sense of community, and deal with prejudice and discrimination at work.

Get Input and Feedback: To make sure the wellness program is fulfilling the requirements and expectations of the employees from a variety of backgrounds, get input and feedback from them. Provide staff members the chance to express their opinions, experiences, and recommendations for enhancing the initiative and developing an inclusive work environment.

Organizations can establish a more encouraging, approachable, and welcoming atmosphere that supports the health and wellbeing of every employee by taking equity and inclusion into consideration during the planning and execution of a corporate wellness program. Organizations may build a culture of belonging and respect for all employees while improving program effectiveness, engagement, and happiness by acknowledging and valuing the diversity of their workforce.

Summary

Establishing a corporate wellness program is a critical first step in helping a firm promote a culture of productivity, health, and well-being. Employers may help their staff members reach their health objectives, enhance their general well-being, and create a happy work environment by putting in place an extensive and inclusive wellness program.

To sum up, the following are essential elements of launching a corporate wellness program:

Needs Assessment: Completing a comprehensive needs assessment in order to comprehend each employee's particular health-related needs, preferences, and interests.

Program Design: Creating an all-encompassing wellness program that encourages inclusivity and accessibility, offers a range of programs and activities, and covers important aspects of health and well-being.

Getting top leadership and important stakeholders to endorse the wellness program and provide funding for its execution is known as "leadership buy-in."

Employee Engagement: Encouraging participation and engagement among staff members by clear and concise communication, rewards, encouragement from peers, and adaptable options for involvement.

Resources and Support: Offering a variety of instruments, resources, and services to enable staff members to actively engage in wellness programs and take charge of their health and well-being.

Equity and Inclusion: Taking into account equity and inclusion issues can help to guarantee that the wellness program is available, pertinent, and inclusive for all staff members, irrespective of their circumstances or background.

Assessment and Ongoing Enhancement: Establishing procedures for appraising program performance, gathering input, and formulating data-driven choices to hone and enhance the wellness initiative over time.

Organizations may boost employee happiness, engagement, and retention while simultaneously increasing organizational performance and productivity by placing a high priority on employee health and well-being and developing a welcoming and inclusive wellness program. A well-thought-out, skillfully executed, and ongoingly assessed corporate wellness program can have a significant impact on employees' lives as well as the overall performance of the company.

THE END

www.ingramcontent.com/pod-product-compliance
Lightning Source LLC
Chambersburg PA
CBHW070210230526
45471CB00002B/908